*Our Flowers*
*& Nice Bones*

# Our Flowers

# & Nice Bones

## Christopher Middleton

Fulcrum Press

## Acknowledgements

Acknowledgements are made to the following periodicals, in which some of these poems have appeared: Burning Deck (USA), Delos (USA), The Journal of Creative Behavior (USA), The Kentucky Review (USA), The London Magazine, New Measure, The Poetry Review, Shenandoah (USA), Stand, The Times Literary Supplement, Transatlantic Review.
Printed in Great Britain by Villiers Publications Ltd London for Fulcrum Press 20 Fitzroy Square London W1.
Of this first edition 100 copies separately printed on antique laid paper and specially bound are numbered and signed by the author.
First edition 1969.

# Note

The title of this book comes from a letter written by Kurt
Schwitters to Raoul Hausmann (c. 1946), in which he described
an event of 1922 in Utrecht: " In Utrecht they came on the
scene, presented me with a bunch of dry flowers and bloody bones
and started to read in our place . . . Nelly lighted a cigarette
and cried to the public, that as the public had now become quite
dada, we would be now the public. We sat down and regarded
our flowers and nice bones " (*Pin*: London, Gaberbocchus Press
1962, quoting Schwitters's original English).

' Found Poem with Grafts 1866 ' and ' A Concert 1866 ' come
from *Hand-Book of French Conversation : Consisting of Pro-
gressive Dialogues on Ordinary and Familiar Subjects*, by M. de
Rouillon (New York 1866). The grafts in the first of these poems
are extracted from Henri Perruchot's life of Cézanne (translated
by Humphrey Hare: New York 1961). The misprint in ' A
Concert 1866 ' comes from the source. The found poem about
Tommy Phelps came from *The New York Times* in 1967.

# Contents

## 1

13 Three Microzoic Nonsonnets
15 Radiation Motif 1
16 The Burrow
17 Day Flower
18 A Topology of the First Telstar Faces
19 Woodpile
20 Lecture Notes
22 Edwards Plateau & Elsewhere
23 Avebury: The Temple
24 Nudes
26 Radiation Motif 3
27 Merope

## 2

31 Uomo nella luna
32 Homage to Kafka
33 Birth of Venus
34 The Alchemist is Preparing the Darkness
35 Two Stone Poems
36 Computer's Karl Marx
37 Lausdeo Teutonicus
38 Milk Sonnet

## 3

41 Mysterious Still
42 The Armadillos
44 Radiation Motif 2
45 The Arrest of Pastor Paul Schneider
46 Found Poem with Grafts 1866
48 TV Masts in Central Texas
49 Victoriana
50 Radiation Motif 4
51 The Last of Mexico 1967
52 Bonnard
53 The Children at Longleat Key
55 Wire Spring

**4**

59 Pavlovic Variations

**5**

67 Lucky Caesar
68 Hans Christian Andersen
69 The Measure
70 The Find
72 Roadside Dreampoem
73 Nothing
74 Shoreham Walk
76 Concerning Revolution
77 Man on the Wall
78 Memory
79 Found Poem
80 The Hero, on Culture

**6**

83 Curbaram
85 The Eagle
87 The Interrogators
89 The Historian
91 The Hermit
93 Salmoxis
95 The Birth of the Smile

**7**

99 The Joke
100 Who
101 Armadillo Cello Solo
102 A Concert 1866 (Found Poem)
103 Ballade in B
105 In the Rain
106 Vivaldi
107 Isla Mujeres

# Three Microzoic Nonsonnets

*for Hans Vogt*

1

Failing: to sit
by the knotted hands
    the night through,

all
    meaningless, as
the backs of words, the black
    cream of moments —

then, on the feet,
to approach
    a door, before switching
off,

    to put straight
a picture on the wall, the hand
    opens . . .


2

Then Goethe, he
says: The old story —
    sea-bed (from

this
    height down upon
Weimar), the whales playing,
    villages now;

what thought of us,
our molluscs,
    had the sea-mew then; yet,
think,

    hear him cross
again this mountain, his wingbeat
    not far.

3

. . . vines, thick with fruit,
moons of pollen &
        the wild rose

    cling,
        I make them, to
the archivolts; lion,
    cathedral snail,

    camel, my loves
make in me
        a room, growing; as light
    swells,

        propels all
night old ribby shadows up red
    curtains.

# Radiation Motif 1

afloat in the windowpane, stuck
in the visible section of tree trunk

like a circular sawblade
the oval breakfast table

supports again objects : the tall
milk bottle, only half full

& a banana, a bunch of grapes
behind the coffee jug, two cups

flanking half a small flower vase —
three globes of blown delicate glass

to bounce, out of the sun,
three windowpanes back to the first one

## The Burrow

Room fanned cool, this curtain
is white, blown to the rondure
of a shell,

they are in me, but anywhere —
tacked to the wall
diamonds
of angry rose, the woollen
god's-eyes, torn from a book
magic fish, a north unicorn :

they feed on the eyes I do not trust,
hearing the air jag
with cicada wings, the latest
day thinly sings out,
old glass —

& with the squeals
of men dying, young,
anywhere, on the highways, old maps,
under helmets,
thinking : Hanoi.

## Day Flower

Sectioned green
stalk, the few
finger-long leaves crinkle

tiny blazon :
four yellow stars
make a lozenge

peopling the silver
membrane
curl
three blue feelers

& all spring
from an ostrich head
jowly green

remote :
blue rounds
the two petals

are palms upped & flat —
why now
bear the weight
of some other universe :

you bring the day flower
the crucified

& leaves flap hallo
as I hold it up.

## A Topology of the First Telstar Faces

*for their recorder, R. B. Kitaj*

Nylon knee & more
a heavenly tan —
calf, ankle, toes dwelling
precious in a boot
of white kid
substitute :

knee & more — not so, curses!
white, a dead
white & thin, pulpy
chicken —

so much hidden
looking
& ascertainable
the dreaded legs

vomit

your syntax of essence
mine as time rolling
unrolling —

a solar
wave, tapering
to spray, filtered
for the skins (infinitesimal)
through the blue
dust-gauze

## Woodpile

Yucca, sheaved
standing blades

& singular
the full moon

shone
this

destruction of green
It is veinless

tough grass
It supports my

shadow kneeling
Woodpile

neat
human oblong

heavy
with flame

## Lecture Notes

white shirt dovewhite flapping clockwork
past through vents in the venetian blinds

voice of the lecturer never to return
baritone white neon overhead in this semi-cellar

voice from under his very particular horn rims
never to return he said & it was Alexander Blok

silver cantaloup back
of Fania's braided head laughs on the other shore

(Blok) crooks of arms pressing doveshapes also
on armrests grained landscape of yellow grandfather

a poem made of everything in the world of fact
I see with my eyes in one instant of time

sunset mystery over the church fence meant symbolic
boundary the model model of his world

even the colour white or was it collar he said
a different something blizzard shirts & ice

spectral changing city Peter the Great I heard
these yellow days pass between the houses & NAZHAKHA

& gulping October 1912 there is a pharmacy
he sighed between every house & the next a pharmacy he said

crowds bloodstain sunset ooze in unstressed ees
composed in dovewhite January 1918

green wicker handbag on the lino with diffuse vowels
eternal battle dream of peace

mathematics on the armrests for skin & swastikas
the whole fragment describing a consonance

my time I will spend I will spend
with a knife I will slash I will slash

died August 1921 in great torment
blackboard Greek triangles

blackboard of chalked Greek triangles

## Edwards Plateau & Elsewhere

The joy these objects echo : to be at grips
with nothing. Upland curlew spans
from Venus to an ear his sporadic
radar treble. Space

rippling through corrugated volumes
of Spanish oak flows & flows
round boles of the black smooth persimmon.
Greyfox through the night barks his lost long cry,

immense sky
floods personality, making all
magnitudes infinitesimal. Ego
(asphalt crawling with vertebrate stunned bees)

a frostflake
cathedral, half
one millimetre flat & two across
blots out webby organisms in the fluting of elm trees :

lavishly, though,
ignoring such phenomena,
pioneers in bed
pumped from the vacuum the genus pinhead,

with laughing hats, big steaks & automobiles :
Jerusalem — Jollyville, built
with powdered mountains in pursuit of ranch-truck wheels
under the eyelid of a foreigner.

# Avebury : The Temple

What these stones are,
stone by stone,
their circle, the road
bisecting it, and the heavy
green earthwork

Night here, gradual stars,
the dew keeps rising
in a mist till the blue
and dark beeches go
for another time another green

We sleep under a mountainous
parsley stick, its rosettes and fans
catching the dew light, and darkening
with the dreams we do not have

All night a murmur and the feet
freezing soundlessly, sleeping bags
damp, not with the tears we do not shed

And at dawn we are walking
under the sweet lime trees, we climb
a gatepost of granite and sit up there

We gaze for horsemen to come,
girls with bacon,
and among grasses for the small flowers,
the far stones touching a remoteness
which is our remoteness, stones
we ask nothing of, as they are revealed

We are revealed in our hands
holding other hands

For once not scared they will come
up the road,
others who do not know what this night is,
who do not care what comes
when the night goes, the night goes

## Nudes

### 1

Ah what have the bunnies & playboys done to us

on a postcard of yore
round moon bottom all naughtiness
nude of yore
I see I see
your big smile of yore
& your rolling eyes wondrous


### 2

In the centre of the room
a vacant cage.
To its bars from walls & corners
jungle grows.

Rubber trees are rising from the floor,
rustling fronds rotate
a web the light sifts through,
becoming copper.
What throbbing eggs assemble
the sonatina of the vines!
And in their midst an old machine-gun hangs,
manned by a parrot.

In the centre of the cage
a boat appears,
and in the boat a girl, asleep,
a nude.


### 3

Absolute altitude
of the golden hairs
planted &
wide

clearings

              underfoot
              the skin
              a bronze
              flows touching
              no horizon


4

When moving
surfaces become spaces.

When moving surfaces
become spaces

who lives in this house?
Groin Smile.


5

No one killed this nipple yet;
happy nipple.

Shoulder, no one broke you;
shoulder white repose.

Peace concave. No one slit
this belly with a bullet.

Sweet to climb, spine, many-turreted:
no one burned you down.

Hopeful woman, like a lake, no,
a sky of smells & wild

ideas balancing
on little toes.

## Radiation Motif 3

Now begins
the straightening of the house

book on the ironing board
bathtub cluttered with shoes
washing a white heap for hours

on the bed &
passports in the icebox
brushing hair

eye in profile absorbs
a torn print column yellowing
horoscope

the head cocked smiling
across crumbs & apples
barefoot

blue air grisly still
with plucked hearts, incessant
harp Mexico

balloons & temples wait for us
our mouths crave
your shape of dust

## *Merope*


Don't let me
chase
the big stone
down the mountain

your laughter
wells
here,
little spring.

## Uomo nella luna

```
mano

luna
rosa

uomo
orbe
nera

mano
rosa
nell
uomo

orbe
nell
uomo
nero

luna
nell
orbe
rosa

uomo
luna
nera

mano
orbe

nemo
```

# Homage to Kafka

```
cage  cage      cage  cage      cage  cage      cage  cage
cage  cage      cage  cage      i     cage      cage     b
cage  cage      cage  cage      cage  cage      cage  cage

cage     r      cage  cage      cage    ir      cage  cage
cage  cage      cage  cage      cage  cage      cage  cage
cage  cage      d     cage      d     cage      cage  cage

cage     r      cage    bi      cage  cage      cage  cage
cage  cage      cage     d      rd    cage      cage  cage
i     cage      cage  cage      b     cage      cage     b

cage  cage      d     cage      cage     b      cage  cage
cage  cage      cage  cage      cage     b      cage  cage
cage  cage      d     cage      r     cage      cage  cage

cage  cage      cage     i      cage  cage      cage  cage
cage  cage      cage  cage      cage  cage      cage  cage
cage  cage      cage  cage      cage  cage      cage  cage

b     cage      b     cage      r     cage      cage  cage
cage    rd      cage  cage      cage  cage      cage  cage
bi    cage      cage    bi      cage  cage      cage  cage

r     cage      id    cage      cage    bi      bird  bird
cage  cage      cage    ir      rd    bird      bird  bird
cage    bd      i     cage      bird  bird      bird  bird
```

## Birth of Venus

THE          iiiiiii          ALCHEMIST

```
THE               iiiiiii             ALCHEMIST
                  iiiiiii
                  iiiiiii
                  mnuyunm
                  iiiiiii
                  iiiiiii
                  iiiiiii
                  iiiiiii
                  miiiiii
                  imiiiii
                  iimiiii
                  iiimiii
                  iiiimii
                  iiiiimi
                  innnnni
                  iiiiiii
                  nnnnnnn
                  iiiiiii
                  nnnnnnn
                  niiiiin
                  iiiiiii
                  uuuiuuu
                  yyuuuyy
                  iiiuyyy
IS                yyyiyyy             PREPARING
                  iiyyyii
                  yyyiyyy
                  uuuuuuu
                  iuuuuiu
                  uuuuuuu
                  nnnnnnm
                  nnnnnmn
                  nnnnmnn
                  nnnmnnn
                  nninnnn
                  nmnnnnn
                  mnnnnnn
                  nnnnnnn
                  nnnnnnn
                  nnninnn
                  nnnninn
                  nnnnnin
                  nnnnnni
                  nnnnnin
                  nnnninn
                  nnnimmm
                  mmmmmmm
                  mmmmmmm
                  mmmmmmm
                  mmmmmmm
                  mmmmmmm
                  mmmmmmm
                  mmmmmmm
                  mmmimmm
THE               mmmmmmm             DARKNESS
                  mmmmmmm
                  mmmmmmm
                  mmmmmmm
```

# Two Stone Poems

1

          s  t  o  n  e

    w    i    n    d    o    w

                  s
                  t
    w   i   n     o         d   o   w
                  n
                  e
                     w

          i

             n

       d          w

                        st

    o
    o

          s  t  o  n  e


2

       s  t  o  n  e

       p  o  o  l

    p  o  s  t  o  n  e  o  l

             o   P   o
          o      l       o
             o        o
                  o

             p

             o

## Computer's Karl Marx

*" . . . how does . . . this reorganization of
production relations actually proceed . . .?"*
*N. Bukharin*

production relations
class consolidates
rioters plot
patriot sailors
pelt iron captains
soldiers postmen
loot old arsenals
rotate tripods
capture police

conscript prostitutes
rusticate prelates
cut pop opiates
stop past increments
start national product
poor labourers
proud as lions
note price reduction

popular action
protect red capital
nouns are tools
stone duct latrines
replace palaces
true cloud snailports!
pleasure in creation!
nice proletariat
not proletariat!

# Lausdeo Teutonicus

monstra
skandalaus
auslös
demonstra

kandala
demondial
ösende
monstrandalaus

onende
dadalaus
skandalos
ionen

mondala
mandalaus
ödelösende
mördermaus

domlose
demonstrata
astralende
monstradom

mondlos
lauslos
lauslösende
skandalauslösendedadademonstrationen

## Milk Sonnet

```
Moooooooooooooooooooooooooooooinds
Moooooooooooooooooooooooooooooove
Moooooooooooooooooooooooooooooinds
Moooooooooooooooooooooooooooooove
Mooooooooooooooooooooooooooooark
Mooooooooooooooooooooooooooooaken
Mooooooooooooooooooooooooooooark
Mooooooooooooooooooooooooooooaken
Mooooooooooooooooooooooooooooeeks
Mooooooooooooooooooooooooooooome
Mooooooooooooooooooooooooooooeeks
Mooooooooooooooooooooooooooooom
Moooooooooooooooooooooooooooooved
Moooooooooooooooooooooooooooooved
```

3

## Mysterious Still

Mysterious still
how the first
warm spring wind

deepens
the town
lanes & doorways

recede toward
caves
of light beyond them

## The Armadillos

You suddenly woke and saw
on the bedroom hearth an apple green
puddle of moonlight. It was the armadillo,
sitting on top of the chimney, put it there;
with his long snout for a siphon, I suppose.

More often the armadillos
perch in the trees. They stare
at each other, count the rings
which buckle them in; or —
they discuss things.

Don't fall, Harriet! Arthur, don't fall!
We can't help it if the armadillos
drop like bombs and catch only
in the lower branches with their claws.
Falling like that, they can't be lonely.

Winters, they leave the trees and trundle
to the end of the valley. In twos and fours
they cluster there and comfort each other.
The frost feels them under their bucklers;
they taste it happening in their jaws.

But in the trees where they build hides
of cardboard boxes and paper bags,
their main concern is believing summer.
For my friends broken by special committees
I hang out armadillo flags.

They run fast and go underground
where silence is, for sending signals.
Or they climb to the tops of telephone poles
and jam the exchanges of political assholes
with the terrible sound of knitting.

If you wake again, do not scare,
but wonder at the armadillos;
they'll be watching us from up there,
winking their neat eyes, arranging their faces,
hoping that something shows.

## Radiation Motif 2

Tree-roach, mantis, moth
cannot come in; huge throbbing sun,
this lamp is not for them —

cling to your window screen,
tremendous extinct immortals:
owl mask & friendly elm
distort our features —

it is long since they came in
(on earth a little space
to bear the beams of love) —

invaded palms discovering the swell
of buttocks, the slow tongue thrust
into the sex, another mouth
open holds the shining phallus —

their terror. We blind it
with a kind of pleasing. No
heavier joy.

## The Arrest of Pastor Paul Schneider

Together, from
    the bed they hear
        footsteps; it
must be (he thinks, today
        and she : ) a dream

my sinews legbones
exploding head
        changed into
    powder, then
cloud, whitest, the gate
    clicking, now
who's there? He can
        hear them

further
    down the hill (& the cloud

a cool in summer,
        roasted) she

to the window

nothing
but the road (yellow curl) stabbing
        to his church

wakes
    him
        the knock
Why (he says) wait
        we're surrounded

## Found Poem with Grafts 1866

To the north-east
    is the park of Mousseaux.
The Baths & Gardens of Tivoli
    & the slaughter-house du Moule must be seen.
Tivoli, near the Chaussée d'Antin
    contains forty acres of ground.
It is quite equal to your Vauxhall by night
    & is much superior in daylight.

But who is the man in the rusty black shapeless felt hat
    pointing south-west?

The walks are ornamented
    with roses honeysuckles & orange trees.
Amid the copses are seen
    rope dancers & groups riding at the ring or playing at
                                 shuttlecock.
All around are arbours filled with people
    enjoying the sight of the various amusements.
There is in the middle of the garden a theatre
    on which two hundred couple might dance at the same time.
There are also artificial mounts from which people descend
    in a species of car with incredible velocity.

But who stands in the huge overcoat that had once been brown
    & now is stained with large green patches?
Who is this in the trousers that are too short,
    revealing blue socks?

There are many canals
    in which the public amuse themselves in boats.
In the evening
    the illumination presents a lively spectacle.
All sorts of dances
    commence then,
& after the vocal & instrumental concert the evening concludes
    with the exhibition of splendid fireworks.

Is he not the man who cooks
    hideous mud in the Rue Beautreillis?

Who says : The day will come
    when a single original carrot shall be pregnant with revolution.
Whose wallpaper groans with addresses in the childish script
    of nudes he throws downstairs cursing through his teeth?
And I am aglow, he says,
    with all the hues of the infinite.

## TV Masts in Central Texas

Two webs, tall,
soaring up, straight & thin,
beyond juniper miles,
and spun,
the distant structures,
so fine what is seen
is the blue
rotunda
which encases them.

This wanes
to black
but their beacons, all night,
slide winking
up & down in line:
beads
of crimson dew,
heads on a totem pole.
The dark intervals pump,

O you lost dream-Indians,
through cathode tubes
our sog of doings: golden
bombers & grins bracketing
soap-brands, always
the mouth will explain them,
the bald
ranked faces watch on,
filling in the time.

# Victoriana

In the gardens of Windsor Castle
walks a philosophic owl;
wingtips clasped over his coccyx,
stooped he stalks, pondering much.

Meanwhile the moon puts pale fire
in the turrets of Windsor Castle:
shut windows halt its gleam,
the queen is pulling her boots on.

The moon is evident also
on the buttocks of stallions grazing,
in the lake without any holes,
in the blood that drips from the owl.

For certainly blood drips down
the philosophic owl:
he leaves a pool on the turf,
wherever he stops to think.

Now the queen comes riding, sag-jawed,
down the long moonlit avenue;
her dead prince gallops beside her
on a very noble ostrich.

## Radiation Motif 4

Toward evening I switch on the sprinkler.
The calyx of springwater frays into silver drops.
Red bird & yellow bird
people a bush the water beads with stars.

Drinking the stars, fluffed-out throbbing bodies,
I can smell you, the wet dust you shiver off.
Your silver whistles come to shape my hearing;
the touch of your claws
tinkles on the leaves.

Absurd. To be so possessed
by the nature of things. What claws,
what creatures of air can take & give
the old gentleness.

## The Last of Mexico 1967

Roadsigns are cleaner,
Most people are taller.
With first-class loot
From a second-class people
We arrived here happy.

Our bowels itch
For the red-roofed house,
Whiter than ice-cream,
Hopefully cooler,
And perfectly certain.

In the long tube flying
Dick wore a wild hat.
Squirts of insecticide
Guarded our genes,
Flagons of Kahlua,

Big pottery doves,
The chocolate crunchers
And genuine gods
Near busted the seams of
Our bags in the hold.

Our profiles are realer,
Our pictures prove it.
Here's one we stopped for:
A cracked old woman
Holding her hand out.
Oaxaca was cute.

We have done our stuff.
Our money is more.
Our President is nicer.
Our c - - ks are longer,
Our c - - ts are homier
Than in that lost land.

## Bonnard

Does the body rest against his eye, the cool
changing its colours : rose, purple, silver
framed in a door, the enamel of a bath

their life the elements dream through,
figures all facing at different angles
do not touch, they include one another —

dwelling on a thing, the eye feeds its boutons
energy sprayed from a few co-ordinates : loaf & horse,
each its own dimension in the starred dream

shields the colours! blue skins,
cocooned girl's crotch, or aloof apple,
a buffoon child, flowers in a bowl

& her face everywhere, turning from a cup
to smile with a mouth like a slice
of baby watermelon, celestial clown girl

or bored, sprawling bare on a rumpled bed,
brown arm thrown across her ribs,
the left hand tilting a small breast —

but where the skin starts it is the idyll
playing out any boundary to scan
throbbing ascensions in the space around,

street dappled with skirts & metal,
woodland blue with edible branches,
crimson billow of a kitchen cloth

it is where the dogs do battle,
canaries roast in evacuated rooms,
the history-makers unload their dead,

hack it to pieces. To pick it up again,
restore it, whole, a lifetime on fingertips
grinding a rainbow from the ignorant dew.

## The Children at Longleat Key

We have gone to the sea at evening.
We float over waves in a rubber tyre.
Your legs are glistening your hair is wet.
My shoulders are cool I hear the ripples.

Orange cloud swells over a thin black line.
We gaze at the water wheeling with rainbows.
We lean back with upturned faces.
Your hair hangs down it darkens the water.

We are floating out to sea we are happy.
On the far white sand are two black dots.
White sand curves a warm banana.
A swept and sharp banana a sword.

We see the two black dots are waving.
Bigger it grows all the sea around us.
They wave and shout we wave and wriggle.
We beat the sea with our feet and hands.

It is a very old man and a very old woman.
Far off he is jumping on the hard sand.
Far off she is brandishing a parasol.
He wears a black hat and she white stockings.

We have ridden the billows and watch the foam.
Soft crystals cling and spit on the rubber.
There are two voices shouting and mixing.
We stand in the water we feel its pull.

It is pulling your knees and you go under.
I catch your feet it is hauling you away.
The little old people walk toward us.
The sand nudges between our toes.

His black hat rim sits level over his eyes.
Her white stockings cover two sticks.
They are saying to us their big worries.
They make their hands go up and down.

We hear the voices we hold the tyre.
Its cool ring slaps to the sand between us.
They walk away in their twiggy skins.
The shrunken faces will speak no more.

They meant it well the old people.
The sea pounds the beach behind us.
Its blue roar begins like a shiver.
We watch them vanish into thin air.

## Wire Spring

I saw the wire Spring come,
the first clock beclambering the redbud;
out of a marble cloud thrush-legs fell
hitting the grass with a twang.

Like a rose through muscle,
like flesh through a wire web,
through the cities & sewage meekly
aromas of bluebell bubbled, coffee & cod.

O the tender new vibrations
of radar marines attentive in airports.
O the nuzzling of sweet electricity
along the intricate barbed fences.

A huge oak harp began to moan & sway,
a phantom ocean of green navels.
The marble cloud was hanging low,
with numerous strikings of twelve.

The first clock said : it is time we killed.
The second clock said : it is time we told.
The third clock said : it is time we have.
The fourth clock said : it is time we kept.

Phalloi enamelling the round of roots,
white & orange & purple, each
with a spring coiled tight in its tucket :
the air shook with their slow tremolo.

## Pavlovic Variations

1

I came to the sea shore to hear speeches about beauty.
Nobody's here.
It still gives the pebbles gooseflesh
merely to think of the metamorphoses :
driftwood sparser, modesty
after all the big words.

I came to the city, back
to the wise & their logic.
Fish met me on the way,
we walked along together.

Sea roads & city roads all lead to the same banquet.
On the table the cuts of sun are transparent & cold.
I keep watch at the gate, to discover who makes the changes in
                                                            things.

I raised my hand, to make sure of the sky :
I touched the breast of a giant bird,
dead, only it had not hit the ground.
Through its eye I saw ships travelling in circles;
an ancient way to bury the sails.
What day of creation is it?

The chair I sit on sinks deeper and deeper into the sand
under the weight of the city I am clasping.
I preserve it in the hollows of my hands like a sip of water,
with few words,
& shall surrender it to someone with fewer
tomorrow.

More & more one loves
the man beneath the sea.

2

Senator Dogface demanded a complete bomb
to rub out the problem on his agenda.
Professor Quorum, on efficient feet, strides outdoors,
behind him a trail of neatly beheaded pupils.

I numbered the pebbles : there were too many.
The sea keeps coming at me, with confusion but no change.

Moving my chair back I turn to the gate :
brown city with choked arteries; a thousand
died on paving stones under four inches of snow,
under four miles of Senator Dogface's blotting paper,
under Professor Quorum's electric pyjama cord.

I keep watch at the gate. Who makes the changes in things?
The cuts of sun thickening multiply,
young pigs & cows go gallivanting —

a summer fish patrolled its pool.
               What night waits for them
with its dioxide oven? On what day
will their creation come?

3

Shining yellow :
                    cyclones
      polish the sea.
                Bald clown
down there, it put a stop
      to your wrinkles.

I was discovering your games :
                        temple columns
shuffled by artillery,
        floating hair of the dancers;
                    flute note remote foghorn
calling through surf-thunder.

The sea from its pocket
      has taken papers : unstamped,
portraitless.
            These tongues are torn from our heads, we pound
at the gates with ammunition & whiskey.

He
walks because he is not stopped by anything.
He considers things
      as points breaking the light for his amusement.

4

Over a splintered pine these blank pages riffle.

From foam the orbiters rising; later, keel tracks,
fisheries; last, the naming of stars. With newborn mouth
a tablet sucked holy milk: I understand

the central nervous system of Alexander. I collect
25 different vine-tip sections in the camote patch. I interrogate
the quiver of needles tracking Mars.
                              I can peel
an orange in 11.52 seconds. I know

nothing. The beat of a heart tears it from the breast
of the giant starry bird. Nobody
is here. Nobody knew

what to do with it.

5

To what space do they belong, the figures torn from a fog
    & what are you? A cathedral. I woke to the silver trickle
from one tap in one hut the twenty of us

    & stood up another day
lidless brimming excrement bucket
    columns & motes tearing asunder the stored deluge of light

200 metres to the bodies we dug out with bare hands
    a snowy braid was widow Lautmann
Pavel's child came to pieces in my hands

    To what realm do they belong, rays modelling
the chevelure of stone, pierced volumes which walk
    my body through transfigurations of the rays, 200 metres more

carting the flesh in barrows
    flesh peeling from bone as we dragged them ghostless
out of the earth to the furnace

    To what region where the forms dwell all day another day
for dragging by the hair we had stroked
    ghostless bundles of flesh bulletmarks in the neck

silhouettes : to what space will the trickle from one tap scrape
    from our eyesockets the memory of that flesh, washing
the smell from our gums with a sip of water

6

There is one who shouts with the shape of himself
last seen
feeding on garbage in the camp near Voronezh

Now I shout with the shape of myself to hear
in the new light the flap of old timetables
platforms I spent the better part of my life on
a solitary overcoat among broken signals
& shall bleed to death on a street between the painted lions

I came to the sea shore to hear a different rampage

The city cupped in my hands I drink its terrible child gaze
Balls of foam blown inland
I found the marble head, butchered its eyesockets
& stare back at the abyss closing & opening
its immense sex

But it is now, at the table, as we whisper with things
under the old lamp that hangs

It is now
over the glass blue pepper-pot that stands, Pavlovic, stands

When we see a grass blade bend in the new light
When we can hear
someone playing a saw over the hill.

*Note: the first section is a translation via German of a poem by the
Yugoslav poet Miodrag Pavlovic.*

## Lucky Caesar

Lucky Caesar,
epileptic,
bald,
the last man
to know
you were crossing
the fish-filled,
Latin-speaking,
real river Rubicon.

## Hans Christian Andersen

Sweet amazing marginalia
to a Denmark as dead
as its parsons. What gloom,
the nineteenth century,
dripping Hamlet's
corpse-fluids. Snowy forests

he entered in a golden submarine;
pale aurora desire,
a sunken god
in tight black boots —

up crowded streets he sped
in Prague,
across the cobbles
bobbing about in a tiny carriage,
shouting, waving & shouting :
" Beautiful girl !
Stop ! I love you ! "

## The Measure

She is going down to the water
restless
& the long hair on her shoulders

the arches of her feet
skinned roots of olive, as delicate,
shape small hollows of air across the sand

Clambering towards her
the sea that knows nothing
the young form, aerial, always cool hands
how do I know her

crossing with swift transition
sometimes, Ionia, your hills

it is the measure
outpacing prediction, we must go
ten thousand miles to the broken statues

## The Find

What to do
here, now
but write

how it is
to wait, in the body
a thing keeps

pounding, biceps
grind,
almost, with

the load of it, no
need to say
who, ever.

To shed it into
an image,
how pathetic. Look :

the hero, no
bigger than
a pin, so far,

he leaps horizons,
triggering acute
crises in nature,

*e.g.*, a man who eats
bats,
the fleas & all,

or a mountain
of a man,
with his ores,

off him cascade
in chaos
glorious adventures.

This table keeps
my legs buckled,
I am hungry,

I am rock,
useless, altogether
useless, but

for waiting.
When you come,
you'll find me

gone, waiting
elsewhere, in
some brooch pin,

or in the glass
you have filled
to drink from.

## Roadside Dreampoem

Mind   bung
   or an ant
     it attacks
the sweet
   crumb; spigot
soupir
   of a city
     far, or near
grasshopper —

I am a sea I am
   a double-
     bass thump,
colossal baby
     cordite, oilfumes
   billow
for life
— for life

   haaaaaah —
shuteye
   snug-as-a-cunt.

## Nothing

Nothing
as it is, you come
from the bath, barefoot
& I see how barefoot

every time
I say this, say that
what goes wrong
is it the time

O barefoot
to hold on
in the silence
you understand

## Shoreham Walk

We walked
up through the wood
nettles & oak
a dark green

fall of light
leading us
past soft
erect wheat

then the white
potato flowers
& flints, a few
rusty can tops

it is the shining
June day, warm
as seldom
in our country

on our skin
a south wind
silver barley ears
are swaying

swaying us
& a lark
less visible than
the flower, blue

big, no bigger
than your pupil
under crusty
oaks again, ferns

they smell of salt
curved seawaves
& a place
we found

called the kingdom
of children
you said, because
nobody frowns

as you climbed
vanishing up
a giant beech, red
as old blood

tall as the sky,
so many strong
branches it
was easy

## Concerning Revolution

All summer the jasmine bush
was billowing
between the house & the forest.
Winter trotted the beercans out, hung
rusting in its ribcage; bedsprings & aspirin bottles
sprinkled under the oak trees.

Why curse
the previous people. At my back door
a scarred enamel pot,
rickety boards :
there is a sea coming in
hides nothing.

In the forest I left a toy
for the spirits; a diminutive
tricycle. By the hole
an armadillo dug I put a warped picture book.
Lest all the old life be wasted
I have kept one tabasco bottle, bent, of clouded glass.

## Man on the Wall

up there, climbing the wall
where he is, we see him
flex the left knee
right leg straighten, right arm
sprung from the shoulder blade
left hand like a fist
of ribs

the flat body so taut
its tallness, all reek & sinew
ignores the feet his
bloody finger ends
& gasps cannot reach

but the wall
neither smooth nor rough
neither brick nor glass
horizon of schist
upright in a reversed
world not a world

there being no roof for it
to taper into
there being beyond this place
which is no place
nothing

& the legs & the arms
slip at the ultimate
tension, like liquid
the whole body subsiding
without thunder
the head out of sight
flipping back, just once
has hammered on something

we have fitted him
into the black bed the black bed
a soft whistling
as the body threshes
under the wool & the linen

## Memory

Hard plank hurting the bones in your bum,
but between them and the Caribbean :
indigo undertow, fanged barracudas.
Sun like sandblast & the stink of shrimp.
Salt fret gnashing the left eyeball.
Endless blue gush the boat chugs through;
unplaceable blaze that aches in the head.

Six yards off, a tiny rose-pooped caravel
always floats alongside
with five proportionate people.
A life contained, sweet music
of sea-harps faintly heard,
swept past the coconut island,
while her soft long hair
rippled over your face, not tickling.

## Found Poem

Tommy Phelps traded grunts
& groans for prayer &
Scripture quotations.
Mr. Phelps, once known as " Nature Boy ",
had long blond hair
& wore tights &
wrestled for a living. Now
his hair is black
& he wears a suit &
he is an evangelist.

## The Hero, on Culture

Shit
On
You,
Mother.
All I wanted was out:
To be free
From your festoons
Of plastic
Everlasting
Christmas cards.

6

# Curbaram

Curbaram says: At present they are encamped outside the walls, and we shall drive them back into the city. From this hill you can count their horses, unsaddled, in the enclosure to the left, also their tents, including the storage tents, which are not round but square. One thousand four hundred and thirty two men spread over an area of one mile: by eleven thirty they will be concentrated at the city gate, a tumultuous mass of armour, horses, elbows and heavy feet. At that time you will stop firing and save your ammunition. They will kill one another as they try to press through the gate. By noon we shall have them inside the walls, and they will see us, crowding these ridges with our camels and artillery. The rocket batteries will be positioned at these three points, northwest, south and east of the city. You will maintain a heavy and constant fire from shortly after noon until the sun sets.

Some of these men will plan to escape from the city after nightfall. They will lower ropes from the parapets, and arrive at the foot of the west wall one half hour after midnight. Probably they will be called Guillaume, Albric and Wido, but you need not concern yourselves with that: besides, there will be others, of whose names I am not yet certain. Well now, these men, about twenty in number, having reached the foot of the wall, will move stealthily westwards, making for the sea. The terrain is not easy. By three thirty their exhausted boots will have given up on them, the soles torn away by the rocks which carpet the entire area west of the city to within half a mile of the sea shore. They will continue to move forward barefoot, then on their hands and knees. By dawn, their hands, feet and knees will be lacerated down to the bones, but they will keep moving, for at dawn they will, at last, get a first sight of the ships. The ships are manned by their own people, sailors from Akra Korakas, Archangel, Florida and Plymouth. Then they will be standing, kneeling and lying on the shore, perhaps even feeling the sea as it cools their wounds and stings their eyes. At that moment, the sailors will up-anchor and cram on sail, for they will be subjected to a concerted attack by our air and sea forces: the galleys from coves north of Port Saint Simeon, carrying archers and cannon, and aircraft loaded with bundles of our widely read literature. The ships will attempt to escape, while they, for their part, will stand on the shore, shouting and waving and weeping with the pain of their wounds and their worstedness. Their ships will consequently be destroyed, as soon as their sailors have seized the opportunity to study our discharged literature.

The men on the shore will then retreat to the low dunes, where, human strength being not easily exhausted in times of stress, they will build a defensive wall of sand, rocks, seaweed and rotten fish. The wall will be fifteen yards long, three and a half feet tall, and two feet wide. It may, even at noon, provide them with a modicum of shade.

# The Eagle

Born among the bleak immensities of the Urals, the eagle rapidly acquainted himself with towered cities of the south, whence issued on summer nights the music of mandolins, and with the cities in the northern snows, made luminous by the lanterns attached to sleighs as they travelled, with much ringing of bells, from palace to palace. His soaring flights took him also westwards, among other peaks, and it was here that his days were defined by the long notes of alp-horns creeping around the bluffs, pouring along the deep valleys, as the breath of some hatless peasant pressed into the brass mouthpiece. These were his first journeys, long journeys: from them he would return to his perch, to gaze down upon the earth below, as if its many layers of rocks and epochs were the staves of his musical score, over which his notations were beginning to spread, and his silences, in amongst and all around the striking of drums.

From the altitude of his flights he was able to discern the streets and interiors of towns hidden in the folds of time: pewter jugs, copper pans, and bottles of ruddy antique glass; Punch on mule-back crossing a cobbled square, and singing, as the sun began to rise, of Silesian girls capacious as barns; a royal courtyard criss-crossed by freshly trimmed trees in which oranges glowed and dancers who sprang from shadow to shadow; in Famagusta, amid celestial flutings, the birth of a waxen-fingered Baby Saint Barnaby reducing to powder the temples of Aphrodite; and Theodora's witty but antecedent rape of a sibilant Dancing Master, Asterius by name, in a nook which housed at that time the celebrated Byzantine astrolabe.

Much later came the period of the interviews. The merest suggestion of a phrase, and he would circle the sky above with expressive swoops, plunge full tilt at his nomad interrogator, and at the last moment rise again with a gentle exertion of his powerful shoulders and vanish in a flash of russet and gold. And yet he bafflingly alluded to his caducity, and to his dealings with physicians and cupboards stacked with pots of jelly. From Ireland and France came the main sources of his sustenance; he refused the excitements of the cactus or of chemical foods and powders from the Orient.

His last flight is still a subject of lively inquiry. From a certain altitude one morning he descended on to the back of a whale, which immediately set out for Tierra del Fuego. The eagle's claws were firmly, if not desperately, planted in the black fat on the back of the whale. The whale kept to the surface for the first day and night, but at noon on the second day it submerged, despite anxious cries from the eagle, and despite the eagle's rappings on the flanks of the whale with his powerful wings. Under the sea, the eagle for the first time saw the shoals of sunfish dispersing like clouds as the whale crashed through them, and, looking back, these same shoals coagulating again as if no more than a breeze had passed. The eagle's only nourishment that day was a young mullet, who had approached the scene mistakenly.

The whale surfaced at night, but by this time the eagle no longer had any memory, his soul absorbed nothing new, except for the rushing of the water as it flowed unendingly over him. Even on the surface again, under that full moon which shone upon the two of them, he knew only this rushing, no longer the nourishing air upon his plumes, no longer the cool gusts that blew among the homely peaks and sustained his circulations and shaped his cries. This new rushing was amorphous, a blue suction dragged the great body ruthlessly into a hole which was too small even for a human hair to pass through. His feathers fell away, and his flesh; but still the claws gripped the back of the whale, and the eagle still followed every motion of the whale, rising and dipping, rolling and winding, on his regular course to Tierra del Fuego. The skeleton of the eagle is still there, the claws rooted in the black fat of the whale, the bones polished white by the rushing of the waters. The beak is wide open, as if uttering a last cry, the last of all possible cries, which is the silence. Whenever the whale rolls, the skeleton swings this way or that, with a slight clamour, something like a rattling, say, of giant leaves against the window in a dry October.

## The Interrogators

It is some time ago now. The pines are wedges of silver, on either side of the road. Fresh snow crunches under the tyres, with their thick tracks, while the road keeps turning and descending, through a country of frozen lakes, a buried country. We left the main road ten minutes ago. Now we are filtering through these layers of green, silver, and air.

There are a few houses, with small windows, hunched under their loads of snow; a smell of woodsmoke, after we have stopped by the low wooden house with the notice outside. These houses cannot be empty, yet we are not being watched, it is too cold at the windows. The people are presumably huddled around their stoves, burning wood, papers; the insignia were the first things to go. They eat from the pannikins on the dresser, a cold potato, sometimes the leaf of a discovered vegetable. Always they carry these pannikins with them, hoping to discover something edible as they walk around. In mittened hands, or attached to belts, knocking their buttocks. The wooden houses, gashed by snow, are scattered under the pines, as if hurled apart by an explosion. The village has no centre, unless this house with the notice is the centre.

There is a desk, with green blotter and an inkwell, several neat bundles of printed forms. On the blotter lies a yellowed sheet of paper inscribed with some lines in sloping gothic script. The room smells, warm, woodsmoke and faint local tobacco, a suspicion of rum, doubtful, but stale, it invades first the nostrils, then the folds of the thick blue material of our clothes. The windowpanes are opaque around the edges, steam inside and frost outside. The transparent centre reveals the road, churned with tracks, hanging boughs of pine, and then the nearest two houses, their dark walls quite suddenly facing away, as if just caught in the act; and the door creaks as a little man steps in, takes his green hat off, and is seating himself at the desk.

He is as trim and brittle as an elf. The green forester's jacket and trousers, the black knee-boots, belong exactly to this body. His face is wrinkled, the white pointed beard wags as he speaks, his eyes are blue ice. The officer facing him is immediately ashamed of his stomach, so large, shamefully large, and he cannot draw it in. Yet he makes the effort, now that he has to draw breath to speak.

Outside, somebody is there. The black shape against the snow, a head enveloped in a scarf, whoever it is he moves to the window, peers in, then abruptly clears off, into a silence disturbed first by his boots, then only by the sifting sounds of the snowflakes falling against the glass.

The forester has little to say, in fact. No, there never were any batteries here. But 35 kilometres north. No, these forests are empty, there was nothing hidden here. We never saw anything like that. The people who live here have always lived here, only one refugee family, from the east. No accumulators. No search-lights. The lake is that way, it is frozen.

# The Historian

Things might not be so bad if I did not always have to write it in a hurry. The historian, after all, should move at a leisurely pace among the objects of his investigation, as a dog might, in a forest of lamp-posts, a lucid dog, that is, one who knows the pleasure of dragging pleasure out. What a magical forest this history has been, even then: first I wrote the official history of the trees, singly and in their concert, the wars, laws, public achievements and transactions, in the manner bequeathed to me by my illustrious forebears. Then, as my hours of sleep grew shorter, with anxiety more than with age, I set about writing the Secret History, at night, as I have indicated, when the servants were asleep in the cellars, only a few shouts in the street below, but still in fear of that man in the black raincoat, belted and hatted, who would one night appear in my doorway and ask, with his smile: " Working late again, Procopius? " — and then I would have no time to stuff my papers under the flagstone beside my littered, but not inhospitable, writing-table.

What more can be said of that girl and the two valets whose tongues were cut out, whose bodies were chopped into little pieces, packed into sacks and dropped into the sea? What of the poet expelled from the city, living now in the woods (with his second wife) — when he told the story of his friend's ludicrous funeral, the coffin too heavy, the factions struggling with flags and wreaths to claim the corpse as an advocate of their particular lies, was he laughing or crying?

I wrote the Histories in order to buy time for the writing of the Secret History. And the Secret History had to be told in a hurry; I cannot exist in this suspense for long, though it can be, for an old man, almost as exhilarating as an early love-affair, all the same. How two-faced one is, especially when facing oneself. The doctor says that I am ill. Yes. They said this of that other poet, in whose will it was written: " Let no man say that I perished because of some sickness during these years. It was their brutality which killed me, the torment of their lies, the fear which stopped my heart whenever a door would creak ".

I remember Theodosius well, not a pleasant fellow, to be sure; but it was an injustice to tie him up in that cell like a donkey, with the tether tight around his throat, four months at a manger, standing there in his excrements. Once he had gone safely mad, they let him go; and he died. I am told that Theodora used to come and bray at him, when she could find the time, lift up her skirts and wiggle her bottom at him; and she had him flogged if he declined to look at her: lack of due respect.

I cannot help laughing when I think of the astrologers whom they mounted on camels and drove through the streets for the mob to jeer at. Old men. Justinian's face is said to turn, at times, into a shapeless lump of flesh: no eyes, eyebrows, nose or anything. To think of that lump buzzing with plans for the killing of thousands. They uproot entire populations, weeping children, the tenderness of old women, worshippers of different gods, gods of the streams, winds, of the earth, and march them at planting-time from their villages into faraway camps of special huts where there is nothing to do but die. No, he does not even plan it. He does whatever comes into the lump, according to the circumstances. In the name of the laws. For the acquisition and storage of riches. For the few and no questions. It all makes the young men and women somewhat more irrational than is good for our society. Our society is probably destroyed, anyhow. Never again to sleep, never again to screw, in security. Was he laughing, or was he crying, that man in his hide-out, when he told the story of the funeral?

It is still mysterious here, still real, here in this room of mine. They are still clattering about down there in the street. Tomorrow the blue dust will go on rising, the new towers along the sea-shore too, built there to shove back the sea which licks at their palaces. The thought still bothers me, that, instead of writing, I might have changed the

# The Hermit

It had been a windy night, the long gusts whistled as they hit the eaves, a distant roaring in the elms, which are immense and extend woolly shadows over my roof in the summer. And it had rained, whenever the wind had given the clouds their opportunity, as it drove them down from the north, across the hills. Dense clouds, but they had passed over by morning, and I woke to find blue sky, a bright sun.

I went into the kitchen and saw, through the window, a horse lying on the rough bermuda grass which slopes to the creek under the elms. In the creek there was a second horse, also lying on its side. The first horse had fallen with its right haunch impaled on a stake to which it had been tied by a length of rope. It lay there, unable to move, breathing heavily and anxiously. I could tell that the stake had driven at least two inches into the haunch; the wound had not bled much, but I could not tell how long the horse had been lying there. The horse in the creek, when I examined it, made a hollow noise which came from the breast, not from the throat. Its breast had been split open; the bone showed in the split, which was long, deep, and clean.

It was necessary to move the first horse off the stake. I fetched a plank, eased one end as far as possible under the wounded haunch, and levered the horse gradually upward. The plank began to bend, but the turf was not too soft and the far end held. Then I pulled the plank to the side and set it against the point of the stake, with the haunch now resting on the plank. Then I tried to knock the stake sideways, so as to pull it out of the ground, but it would not budge. I brought thick rags from the house and placed them between the point of the stake and the underside of the plank.

The second horse could not be moved. It was lying across some rocks in the creek bed. From here I had once looked up the slope: the distance had been much greater, the grass glowing in a dark kind of sunlight, as during an eclipse, and the house had taken shape up there, three rooms, books, a green floor. There was no way, even, to make the horse comfortable. It had evidently been hit by a truck; the truck had careered on through the night, perhaps the driver had not even known that he had hit something. The horse was hardly breathing now. And the first horse had been tied to this stake by the rope, which had given it just enough freedom to graze. The rope was still knotted around its neck. I could see that the hooves had become entangled in the rope, which was why the horse had collapsed, in its oppression, on the stake. The wound was a large hole, the dark red insides of it had been exposed as I was levering the haunch clear of the stake.

Both horses were of a deep brown glossy colour. I put my hand to the soft hollow under the left ear of the horse in the creek, stroked it and said, for no reason: " It will be all right."

# Salmoxis

Salmoxis is an obscure barbarian god. Yet the rituals which honour him, as well as his supposed nature, are matters of more than passing interest. It is among the Thracians that he is worshipped. Some say that he will provide for all desires, and that he sees to it that Thracians are immortal — not all Thracians by any means, but at least the Getae, whose towns speckle the north coast of the Black Sea. These two functions — provision for desires and assurance of immortality — indicate that Salmoxis is a beneficent god. Such gods, freakish as they are, remind us of people who think of others and who may even set aside life and time for the good of others. Yet the rituals conducted by the Getae do not indicate this at all. Once every four years the following ceremony takes place. A messenger to Salmoxis is chosen, twelve men stand in a close-knit group with spears pointing upward, the messenger is seized by the arms and legs by four other men, and he is swung three times, at the fourth swing they let him go, high into the air, and he lands on the points of the spears. If this kills the man, then he is an acceptable messenger to Salmoxis. If not, then the other men tell him just what they think of him and they let him go bind up his wounds. This is a curious and cruel ritual. Why not drop the man on the spears from a cliff, or from an elevated rock, or even from a tree? No doubt there is an element of chance in the ritual performed, and another method might decide the issue less provocatively and less playfully. There are, however, other reasons for the ritual. The counting is evidently important, especially the letting-go at the count of four. The importance of the counting can easily be seen, once one has examined more closely the nature of Salmoxis.

Here a legend is helpful. The legend says that Salmoxis came from Samos. It also says that he was originally, or provisionally, a man — and not only a man but a freed slave. It also says that he had been a slave in the house of Pythagoras before he came among the Thracians. The last point is disputed, on the grounds that Pythagoras is too recent; but there is certain to have been another Pythagoras, otherwise Salmoxis might not have existed. At all events, when Salmoxis arrived among the Getae, he was a wealthy man. Nobody knows how he acquired this wealth. He built himself a large house, to which he would invite men with whom he had struck up an acquaintance; over and after meals in this house Salmoxis would expound to the men his theory that men are immortal, evening after evening, night after night, until his guests fell snoring to the floor. Finally, one of his guests, who had often heard the lecture and knew all the variants, asked Salmoxis to prove it. This was the moment for which Salmoxis had been waiting; it happened in the fourth year of his life among the Getae. When his guests had gone, Salmoxis moved with a lot of food and drink into a subterranean chamber which he had been constructing. The next day came, and no Salmoxis.

The Getae were surprised, but they went about their work as usual, once the surprise had led, as usual, to shrugs, head-shakings, and other gestures of barbarian indifference. For three years, no Salmoxis. Punctually at the start of the fourth year after the night of his disappearance, Salmoxis rose from the dead and strode into the market-place. He raised his arms and declared: " Here I am! " Nobody paid much attention to him, in spite of his dazzling white and freshly starched robes. An old woman selling grapes looked up and away again, not even turning down the corners of her wrinkled mouth. A small professor of horticulture walked by, hesitated, put fingers to his forehead, then trudged on his way to the vineyards covering the sunny slopes to the north of the market-place. Again Salmoxis spoke his words. Again nobody took any notice. He retired once more to his house, and wondered what to do now, since this first proving of immortality had not been much of a success. No sooner had Salmoxis entered his house that the entire market-place was bustling with activity, a tumult of wives and boys, the men running and waving their arms, women crowding the lanes and chattering like gannets. Eventually it was decided that the first response had been the best one; and this was adopted now as policy — to ignore Salmoxis whenever he might appear, to have no more dealings with this dull slave morality of his. And so it came to pass that Salmoxis, after four days, duly left the town and was not seen again. There is a slight possibility that Pythagoras, too, had freed Salmoxis in this way, though he took the precaution of providing him with ample funds.

To this day, when the Getae find one of their number who does not live for the day, does not gratify his own desires without hope or fear, when they find that he is dull and talks about himself too much and too long, they wait for three years to give him time to mend his ways, and, if he does not mend them, on the first day of the fourth year they swing him, one, two, three, and on the count of four they float him up into the air, to land, with a chance of life and a chance of death, on the points of their spears.

## The Birth of the Smile

There are three legends about the birth of the smile, each relating to a different epoch. It is the custom to tell these legends in a reverse chronological sequence, as if this might hopefully point toward an ever-receding antiquity with secrets which may one day be told in legends that still have to be discovered.

The first legend concerns the Sumerians. These people came down from the mountains to the plains, in search of food and water. After several centuries of food and water they became bored with the flatness of the plains, pined for the ancient exertion of striding up and down mountains, and decided to build a mountain of their own (there could be no question of returning to the old place). For ten years the men laboured at the mountain. It was the priests who put the finishing touches to it — drilling weeper-holes, planting a tree on top, fashioning chambers inside, near the base, for library materials and, inevitably, a toilet. While the priests were getting busy, an enormous sheet, woven during these ten years by the women, was draped around the mountain. Finally, everyone assembled; and then the mountain was unveiled with due ceremony and with a great beating of gongs. As the sheet sank to the ground, the strings having been cut by some excessively large pairs of Sumerian scissors, the mountain stepped fresh and naked out of its veilings, and all the Sumerians smiled for the first time. This was a short smile, all the same. The Sumerians had built a mountain to walk up and down, a mountain of the heart, a mountain of despair, a mountain of pain; but their smile disappeared when the officiating priest, from under the tree at the top, declared: " This place is a holy place; for whom it is intended, do not ask. And do not enter or climb around on the outside either, or you will die."

The second legend tells that the smile was born on the face of the first woman when she stood for the first time before the first man and perceived the silence with which his phallus grew and rose at the pleasure of her presence.

The third legend tells of an epoch which must have preceded that of the second, if only by a few days. This is what the legend says. When the shaper of life was making men and women, he was careful to give them strong contours to contain the spirit in them. There was always the danger that these forms might dissolve into the flowing which goes through all things. The spirit raged in the new beings, wrathful at being contained, and after mighty strain-ings and heavings it burst out in fire. The fire streamed from the bodies of the creatures and all creation might have been consumed, had it not been for a cool god who took the spirit in hand. Sud-denly he was standing there, in front of a girl. As they faced each other, an island of coolness was created in the midst of the burning. As he gazed at the girl, he began to marvel at her lightness and grace, and at the diaphanous body from which the fire was spread-ing in great lashes. The god spoke divine words to her body, as he gazed in wonder. While he was speaking, the spirit overheard these words and for the first time began to grow content in such a dwelling. That was when the girl smiled. In those times, a smile was simply the consent of the spirit to dwell in us.

If older legends are ever discovered, they may explain to us the terrified smile of Kafka; or the smile inserted at the corners of Ché Guevara's mouth by the thumbs of his murderers.

## The Joke

nun found nude on dunes
nun found stunned on dunes at noon
nude nun found stunned at noon
nude nun on dunes had been stunned & screwed

who saw nun stand scanning dunes?
who stunned nun?
who denuded stunned nun?
who screwed nude stunned nun on dunes?

what had nun done from nine to noon?
was nude nun heard humming tune?
what tune did stunned nun hum?
was nude nun turned on?

stunned nun not screwed : was queen
nude nun smiles : I am a queen
stoned queen stunned self on dunes
queen staged nude stunned nun come-on

## Who

Who is she,
dressed
all in black, the woman
who floated from your naked waking body,
whispering Remember me Remember me

Now she comes
at us,
now, with her soundless pigskin
telephones, running in dreams down roads,
& as we wrestle with our shirts off

Cloudy bird,
perched
on my shoulder & piping she is
the tunes & words I cannot compose.
This dragon-keeper, who travels

with guitars
& cobras,
whose drumming tightens around us
her moss of blood & 3 A.M. kisses,
burns with exhilaration our unique bones

Dark Venus
under the golden hair,
be
merciful to her, & if torment you must,
torment me

## Armadillo Cello Solo

```
didl   dodl   dadl
o      aro       ma
miomar  miodaar
a      dio       da

    oom     oom

a      mor      id
odlm  mamdl  id
o      mal      or
a      dio      ia

        oom
     didl  dadl

dodl   dadl   didl
a      dio       id
miomar  miodaar
malamormalamor

        oom
     malamor
```

## A Concert 1866 (Found Poem)

After the overture were performed successively
    several pieces, well adapted to display
    the talent of Mr. B and Mrs. S.
The duet in the first act
    was very beautiful.
It was encored
    from every part of the house.
We also had the pleasure of hearing Madam P.

The second act began
    by a grand symphony of Haydn.
The adagio was eminently
    well executed.
The violin concerto was deficient in melody, but
    it was executed with great brilliancy by Mr. .......

Finally, after the most admirable of all overtures,
    the master-piece of the human mind in that kind,
    I mean the overture of the Flauto Magico, of Mozart,
The concert concluded by a chorus of Glnck,
    which produced a sensation I cannot describe.

## Ballade in B

BE

BE

TEN TON TONE
BE

           VENT

           HE
           OVEN
           HE

OVEN
HE

BONE BENT ONE TONE
                VOTE VETO
VOTE
NO NO NO HE HOE ONE OVEN VENT

VENT
NET

               THEN BEET
               NOTE

          HEN TONE HE HOE ON ONE TON
          TON HE TONE ON ONE HEN BONE

OVEN HE
TEN TON TONE

BOTH
BENT

BE
          ONE TENT NET BONE
          NO NO
NO NO NO

NOTE
BEE VENT ONE ON VETO TONE
BOTH BENT

          TEN TONE HEN
          TEN TON VETO

BEEN BEET
TONE BEEN
          HE HOE
          BET ON HEN

BET ONE ON BEE BONE

BEE
BONE

ON
ON

NOTE

        BEE BONE
ON

OVEN HE TEN TON
TONE
TONE
TEN TON OVEN TONE

NET
        ONE BENT BONE TONE
        HE BONE
        HE

ONE BEE TONE BE THE THEN TEN TON TONE
VOTE NONE
VETO

VOTE NONE
NONE

BE BEEN BOTH HE HOE THE TON TONE
HEN ON OVEN OVEN ON HEN

        THE TONE
        VENT
        THEN

BEE BONE
BEE BONE
BEE BONE
BEE BONE

## In the Rain

a wee
ogre, he
knows what:

grows
a net?
wears a knee?

*Nyet!* a great
hot
goat to eat

hot
roast
goat

is what
he knows —
with grog got

(*ecco!*) a week
ago from
a wet negro

## Vivaldi

In the bird-throat,
silence.

Venice glacial dome,
in the dawn-light, rippling.

Delicate moving labyrinth,
plucked by the temperatures :

transfix it.
The canals

blacken; this oval
whirling, whirling

in the palace of air; this
lidded minim

hopes, like a child,
for snow.

O, the dark
day.

## Isla Mujeres

1

On one deserted tip
a temple
indelible tanned people
                              Ocean
                                        Ghosts

At the other, Mexico
of guitars
              revolutions
                              camelias

Reek of urine & fish
                    the great garbage tub upended
over a powdery mile.
                              Fishing smacks

Leak essential oil & men living
off hunger.
                    Under the coconut palm
                        pointed boots
                              of a guitarist

Can't get the tourists to pay him anything
                                        for a voice
sobbing of love
                    and the spiderwork
of ten
delicate fingers.
                    Caribbean
blue rippling hot
                        fat mammas
folded into hammocks

And nothing
happens except
Americans

Depressives inspecting the silence
or skindivers festooned
                              with cameras & gum.

2

Well before nightfall
El Circo Modelo, with bent gramophone records
& six tons of static the devil's fart
digs into your skull its permanent icepick

                    Run to the sea
with split ears (in the sea
there is no silence), to the garbage can
& clap the lid on (there are no garbage cans).

In hell I appoint a place for Mexicans
where the silence is holy & perpetual

And the slow trapeze
act of Norma Ramirez repeated
repeated *ad*

*nauseam* will not haunt my more exacting dreams:

for the guitarist
one hundred pesos to get out of the place
with breakfast:
                    magical kick
in the devil's ass, or a cork
to blow him skyhigh when the pressure mounts
(there is no pressure). Juan Manuel

                    Time you were gone
down the dead straight road
past squat brown cottages
of stick & thatch & Indians rotting
in the ocean of Coca Cola.


3

Ramirez bellowing for ever
*sensacion olimpica parte artistica
de la programa*, was he
        holding his nose? It sounded
like all 27 veins in his cabeza
                    would explode

                    Gusts from stars
Pythagoras,
great heaps
of broken triangles
        block the doors,
                        nothing

Nothing doing murmur VIX KABAAL / what
is your name : & the hammock

                    grotto rocks
                    a small cobweb
                    hole through emptiness

What, though, if these
dragon organs, trumpets, yelps gushed
                                from radios
        to lure back the grim
discarded gods, crush
                            the solar fruit
            silence
                    between galaxies & this disc :

Yucatan innocent dream
a different people, eyes
    in their chins, gull-wings flap
for ears, a people
            of dancers whirled fins
drumming
ovations for everyone. And always

the same human wave grinds
down the shores with its blood & sputum

                    Inert norm
invading every grain of antique caracol
& pore of puffing skin.
                        The same hands
grab, the same guts
            to be filled —
                    your ghost

fat Guillaume

Porthole blue zero.